Ramble

Jamie Surrey

BookLeaf
Publishing

India | USA | UK

Presentation by *BookLeaf Publishing*

Web: www.bookleafpub.com

E-mail: info@bookleafpub.com

ISBN: 9789357447898

First edition 2022

DEDICATION

To Pai, The Love of my life.

You've brought me further than my wildest dreams.

"I shall not die but live..."

ACKNOWLEDGEMENT

I would like to thank you, the reader, first and last. Your support means everything. Secondly, I would like to thank BookLeaf Publishing and all involved in the challenge for presenting this opportunity. Jaya specifically for being my publishing consultant, and for your patience and understanding.

Thank you to the Cummings family for sharing your home, your stories, and your music. Thank you David Devine for your love and support; Danielle Craven for your encouragement, and my other friends such as Alex and Kat; Jake, Kay, and Tony; and Maxum. Your friendship and acceptance is precious.

Thank you Lauren and Jayme for your care and support.

Thank you to my teachers who believed in me even when I was small.

To my family, I acknowledge your undying support in my dreams.

PREFACE

Trigger Warning: familial abuse, suicidal thoughts, swearing, mental illness, police brutality, racism, homophobia/transphobia.

Some poems are portraits, some are convictions, some are experiences.

Poetry

Who can tame heaven
And whisper the voice of hell
Comforter of soul?

Speak to me of all
Love, Rage, Grief, Peace; any one
Without a sound.

Condense me, my love
Into a loud symphony
That only we hear.

Let your song echo
Outlasting kingdoms, gone
Beyond time itself.

To condense my love
Voices of gods locked away
You: the voice I lack.

To try to contain
Even Death could never do
You subdue the Earth.

To put it simply
Your voice is roaring waters
Uttered without a breath.

It Wasn't Abandoned

There's a house they call abandoned
With whispers as they pass.
It has no roof.
No door.
Windows long, long gone.

But we saw a light.
And a coat.

"Cheap things"
Trying to keep the rain out.

The Drunk, Drunk Gossip

I don't know how we started, talking about him.
The drunk.
He walks around sometimes..
I forget his name,
But the people here know him;
He's been around for so long,
Wandering the streets begging.

I don't know why, but there was laughter
While talking about his unshaven beard.
His ugly
Unclean
Shaggy, mangy beard.
Gave him a face that could scare someone
And it did.

Scared a tourist pale.
My old relative saw
And told us
How the fancy lady came with her skin white
and sick
Asking if my old relative knew the strange man.

She said she did, it was her neighbour.
Did he scare you?
Yes he scared me! The lady cried,
He tried begging from me!
Oh but he wouldn't hurt anyone, my old relative
said,
He's harmless.

I believe her.
Though my mom and I saw him one night.
He was walking slowly, step by lonely step.
Had an umbrella, opened and closed,
Opened and closed.
He was lost..in a fog.
He was drunk.
So of course we were scared stiff.

I don't know why but there was laughter
Talking about the poor man.
"Oh I laugh, but I pity him!"
"Let's sing more songs,"
"He can sell tickets and beg!"

A Sobrinha de Lucia

I see her everyday. People come in lines, but on
the days there aren't any I can see her through
the window.
It's only for a second as my mom drives past and
I'm in the passenger's seat.
But I can see her old, worn face. Melancholic
and matching the black outfit she wears every
single day.
She's Lucia's niece (so they say anyway). I
believe it, as much as I don't believe that Lucia
saw Mary if God said His Son was our Savior
And He was enough.
But because Lucia saw something, and she's
dead.
They condemn her niece to a life
Of sitting.

Avô — Bolacha Maria

He thought we were leaving.
Everytime we come he makes sure to give us at
least one Bolacha Maria;
Sometimes two, and he always offers more,
saying he has more
He sure does, because when he thought we were
leaving for the plane
He took us to his room, and pulled out of his
drawer
A pack of those crackers.
They were old, softened.
My grandpa ate them heartily because he gave
some to us.
Time had softened them from breaking.

We didn't know what to do.
My mom offered to take my crackers and throw
them away because they were stale;
She'd pretend to be going to the bathroom.
So she left, but my grandpa was not done.
He opened his closet, and had shelves,
Hidden packs, more and more

He dug through every coat pocket
Every shirt pocket
Every opportunity
Any chance
My hands were flooding with the sweet crackers
And he always continued "I have more! I have
more!"
And he wanted us to share them with the family
With the great-granddaughters he had never met
except in pictures.
Who didn't know that he existed, but that he
loved them.

I remember he used to offer me money I didn't
want,
Or an education I didn't need,
But now he knows. . .

For a man who has nothing left to give
Love is
A soft
Stale
Cracker.

So with every visit
He hands us a cracker
Offering us more.

Erin --- The Ivory Sea

I hear her plunge into the quiet sea
And watch curiously above the dry.
Her hands scatter like spiders and loud bees
Winds blow gently over the water's cry.

I see the surface and think what hero
Could carve such sweet soul from so stubborn
stone?
Yet somehow she bends them as agile bow
And strikes the mark to a slow, somber tone.

Erin, you chase the foam of the sea wild
I have watched you drown under the cruel wave.
But then like the sun you rise a child
Taming the ocean behind bars so brave.

My dear, never forget the raging storm.
The lightening blasting, your faith run so sore.
But still--
You shame Apollo more than before.

Modern Racism #1

I work in the city
And everyone fears for my life
Worried parents and their children
"It's a dangerous area"
"There aren't enough cops"
"Twenty years and the city is the same."

I know what they're really afraid of.

Traitor's Guilt

You've been used and abused and misused
But you must keep your mouth shut.
He might kill you.
We might kill you.
Be loyal
To you blood.

So you suffocate as you try to confess
The things we did to you.

It's in the past.

All of our traumas so intertwined
If you love us
You'll keep your mouth shut.

9/11 Monuments

A flock of pigeons fly,
A monarch butterfly flutters;

But the water is trembling.
In thin, undistinguishable lines.
They fall down the cliff, until finally
They burst into tears
And hit the ground
Crackling white.

And a calm sets in as they descend
the stone, black pit,
Gently like snow.

A Mother's Love

I love you.
I love you more than anything else in the world.
I love you so much I'll
Make sure you know exactly as I do
Think as I do
Believe as I do.
I love you so much my little doll-
Why are you frowning?
Why are you saying your love is an obligation?

A Haikyu

Sure, all lives matter.
That is, if you stop killing
Small brown kids.

Beloved Brother

I have seen the basement of your heart
Where the shadows of your soul dwell hidden.
You see beasts dart, a sacred art
Monsters crawling on walls forbidden.

I too have seen them, but I feel no fear
Because the creatures are scared children.
Those are my bones and unwiped tears
Tender dear, you are not a heart barren.

I have seen behind The Phantom's mask
A face beautiful, Beloved Brother.
Cast off your chains, simple ask--
Your footsteps comfort me like no other.

Dearest love, you have my heart in scores.
O' friend, my soul is forever yours.

Moose and I are Nonbinary

An intersex cat
Is not a "he" or "she," right?
If organs matter.

So then can I ask
For you to call me a "they"
When you bend your rules?

My cat was born both..
A vagina and penis
So they are a they.

But you insist huh?
"He's a he, looks like a he"
Hypocritical.

Which is it then, hm?
If my cat "looks" like a he
Can I be a they?

;

Have you ever felt the adrenaline rush of crying
so much you're laughing as you're
panting--hyperventilating and your foot slams
deeper and deeper into the gas pedal as that one
thought of common sense tells you to stop--slow
down--but you crank up the music on max
instead on a blurry, dizzy, rainy night where
everyone is on their high beams and you can't
see shit but you're just laughing and fasting and
begging to go faster to run away from the
thought of--

Religion's Guilt

Her lips as soft as morning rose petals
Cheeks glowing a burnt bronze as her hands
Stroke my face and she falls into me
Collapsing and I feel her curves including
The ones she thinks she doesn't have and gets
embarrassed of.
But in my arms she is safe and in her arms I'm
In a garden of flowers collapsing
Collapsing collapsing
Breathing breathing and breathing
In her breath.

We curl into bloom.

I'm going to lose my mom.
I can't even tell my grandma my real name.
It's too much to ask you to use it either--
I mean I tried, but calling me dead is easier
For you.

You don't want to lose me so
You refuse to see me.

...When I get my girlfriend

Will you see her?

...I love God
But it isn't enough for the church.

Just Give it Time;

To your younger self
Lying there wanting to die
Drink of life first, dear.

Valuing yourself
Will hurt. But if you practice,
It is medicine.

You are the rainbow
Smiling in the rain and sun
Waiting for flowers.

Patience is bitter
But you will love yourself more
Than a moth loves light.

You will love yourself.
You will love yourself.
You will love yourself.
Be honest,
You only hate yourself
For not being what everyone wanted.

A Tribute to King Lear

Love, treated as nothing more than nothing
Bursts, changes -- turns shadow's wheel
As natures rot, and we see something
Of a fool reel, enthroned sub-fate's seal

Oh, poor king--devils cut thy train in half
Eyes blind by words of flattery and pride
Now nothing, cry at thy prophet-fool laugh
As thou runst to the wind, cower--hide

Storm, rage as you weep; revenge comes
So sweetly off thy lips, so roar
Madness, roar! Settle oh drums
Loud scores cry; on thy wings soar
~-~
Mighty king! Hold thy daughter in arm
As she sleeps: tender n o t h i n g to harm.

The Fellowship of Role-Play

Once a week we gather our fellowship
To play a little game of life or death.
One rises a god, and plots our hardship
As the others navigate under fate's breath.

You know who you are, Leo my dear friend!
A fierce flame burns in your bastard spirit.
Son of a bitch! We kin to the end!
Quite the charming bard, sing a song dammit!

Nyah, you with the ever-changing hair.
No ocean could fathom the depths of you
Strong, loyal barbarian; at your glare
The world tumbles before the fight ensues.

And to complete our unity, Tyler
A magic-caster's heart glowing alight.
The light from you makes the stars expire
Conjurer, you have foes die at the sight.

We all take turns; to play, to narrate.
But I cherish the stories we create.

We Are The Book-Keepers

We are the book-keepers; sellers, dreamers
Watchers of the seasons and the stars.
We are navigators for the travelers
Weary from their climb to the top of mars.

Our house overflows with the light
Of artists, poets; makers of story.
Of scientists, linguists; studiers of sight
Of the human eye's knowledge of glory.

Seas froth, winds bellow wild
Forests bright with sun and moonshine.
And we remain in our cosmos wild
Galaxies dance in our hands of book's twine.

We are the book-keepers, I said before
Dreaming behind the desk, forever-more.

Thank You

To you the reader who read the ramble
Thank you so much for entertaining me.
What did you think hm, was it a gamble
Choosing to believe o' so small a fee?

I am a strange mind, very self-conscious.
Did I risk too much, not write good enough?
Are these words of someone too pretentious?
Not having room for more is rather rough.

But this isn't about me, it's all you!
You are here, you stayed, you saw something.
Imagine hands could reflect someone who
They've never seen nor heard, but our truth
rings!

Thank you for staying, and seeing some worth
Stranger, you are the greatest gift on earth.